DREAMER, SMOLDERING

COLLECTED POEMS

E.M. Trotier

BookLeaf
Publishing

India | USA | UK

Dreamer, Smoldering: Collected Poems

© 2021 E.M. Trotier

Presentation by *BookLeaf Publishing*

Web: www.bookleafpub.com

E-mail: info@bookleafpub.com

ISBN: 9789358739183

First edition 2021

DEAR READER

I never thought I would ever write a book of poetry, or even consider binding a collection of my scribblings into something people other than friends and family might see.

But then I decided to take a chance.

Writing this collection has been an incredible journey, and through it I've found a love of having a daily writing practice. This is a record of my journey in learning how to put myself into words that are more than just spilled ink on paper.

I hope you enjoy these poems as much as I enjoyed writing them, and I hope you, too, one day find a way to ignite.

E.M. Trotier

To my sister and all my friends who supported me in the process of writing this. Most especially to my friend Alex - thank you for reading my poems each night. I couldn't have done this without you, my contemporary.

1. DREAMER, SMOLDERING

Dreamer, sitting under a tree on a sunny day,
Dreaming away
The time and place, pretending
That time is neverending.
And that possibilities don't slip away like water,
That our steps will never falter.

Dreamer, eyes aglow with visions like embers,
Forgetting all the many Decembers,
In the warmth of the light.
As if it were not a fight
To set things aflame, oh dreamer remember, trees
Need water and light and food and still there are no
guarantees.

Dreamer, take a step forward.
You don't have to follow the path that was ordered
But nothing will be gained forever standing still,
Hesitating; the world will just turn around you until
You've got something to prove,
You've got to make a move.

Dreamer, awaken.
Open your eyes and see all the paths never taken,
Seize it in your grubby fingers.
There's no telling what lingers
After death,
So take another breath.

Dreamer, ignite.

2. AFTERMATH

That's all well and good, but
How does one take pen to paper, put words to what
They're thinking in a way others can understand?
Getting up wasn't the trouble, it's learning how to land
On your feet and keep running.
I'm not sure if I'm cunning
Enough to keep up the pace,
But deep breath, it's not a race.

3. CRYSTALIZE

Words don't crystalize in my mouth.
I throw them out
Before they can dissolve on my tongue,
Forgotten. I've never sung
Anything made of stained glass,
It all pass-
-es before I could try,
Best to just let it fly
Past my lips and land
In the palm of my hand.

4.   PERPETUAL MOTION

In the absence of air resistance

Objects don't slow down.

In the absence of the trappings of daylight,

My mind spins aroun-

-d without hesitation,

Taking the pieces of my memories and weaving

Them into new shapes, taking advantage of the darkness

To move unhindered, leaving

Impressions of beauty that fade in the sunrise.

5. WAITING MODE

My brain isn't wired right
Some days it's a fight
To get unstuck, I don't understand
How this can still happen, I had everything planned
Out perfectly to avoid it
And then I still get hit
With *please wait, please wait, please wait*

6. TRANSFORMATION

How does one take the hum in their chest
And pin it down, a still-glittering ribbon?
It never looks the same compressed
As it did in a dream, open and endless.

How to take the beating of my heart and turn it into a
metaphor,
Crack open my ribs like wishbones,
Turn them into a shore
With waves of more than blood breaking on the sand.

7. CARSICK

I forgot I get carsick now,
Tried to write poetry but my head forgot how
To deal with the smells and the motion,
I can feel it at the base of my skull, turning like the ocean
Waves. Had to put the notebook down
And stare out the window, try to tune out the sound
Of her music. It isn't so bad, watching the clouds
And the landscape roll by, better than being crowd-
-ed out by buildings or screens. After all, it's not inscrutable
The world is beautiful.

8. LECTURE HALL

Time
D   r   a   g   s
On,
Sandpaper against my skin
Chains around my limbs,
Holding me still.

I twist
And twist
And twist
The rubber band around my fingers,
Tangle it on each hand
But each slowly passing minute is a brand
On my limbs, I can hardly stand
The stillness.

My entire body a taut string
Poised to snap or break free or spring
Out of my seat,
Kept here by the tension, my feet
Slowly, deliberately tapping, quiet
When I want to be loud. I don't buy it,
This idea that stillness is focus
This
Stillness stings me.

9. IDEAS

A burst of light, a spark of life
I grab the shining thread and spool it out greedily before it
can slip from my fingers
But in moments it crumbles from my touch
Ash in the wind

10. STABILITY

At an art exhibit once I saw something that captivated me
Took a hold of my chest and said
Look at this, see
These shreds

Strung up as a web?
I was a mere insect,
This place could become my final bed,
I didn't expect

To see something so fully
What I had been searching for.
It was something holy.
It didn't bore

Me to stand for nearly an hour, staring into the light
With no sense of the passage of time.
For once it wasn't a fight
For stillness, this sublime

Setting seized all the churning gears in my heart
And externalized the cacophony
So it didn't have to be a part
Of me.

Within moments I knew
This was what I was trying to be,
A breakthrough
That made all my pieces agree.

I had long ago accepted
Chaos would always exist
But this image perfected
Everything in my midst.

It was light, sound, color,
An ever-shifting black-and-white projection against the wall
The web taking the clutter
And holding it all

Together. It felt like ocean waves
Rushing off my legs, but without
The sand crumbling under my feet, the ways
You have to work to stay upright as the water moves about

You, no, there was a structure, stability
To hold me secure,
I didn't need agility
To stay sure

In my footing. I could just ride the water.

11. JOY

Joy is a fizz in my chest
It bubbles up out of me until it needs
A release, it gets pressed
Out into the motion of my limbs, leads

To a hum spilling out of my throat
A note
To match the world, bright and glittering.

12. WRITING IS THINKING

I write a poem early in the day
To set my mind a-spinning
While the hours go astray.
Then when the evening comes I'm brimming
With ideas, and my pen begins to play.

13. WALK ME HOME

My friend, walk me home.
It's been so long since I've seen you, I'm in no hurry to be
alone
Again, I'm soaking up your company,
Let's linger at the door and be
The reason the night grows too late.
We have the time, let's not let the weight
Of the hour grow too heavy on our shoulders.
The night is getting colder
And the hours run away, but I don't want to let you go
Yet, let's just let our walking pace slow.
There's plenty of places we can roam.
My friend, walk me home.

14. HARBOR ME

On days like today I want to build a blanket fort.
Take my ship out of these turbulent, nauseating waters, head
back to port
And set my bones on solid ground.
Create a smaller space, filled with the sound
Of soft music crooning quietly out of speakers or through
earbuds
As the syrupy, steady sound floods
Through me, washing out the tangled pain squeezing me
tight.
Let this calm touch hold me tighter so I don't fall apart, don't
have to stand quite
So stiff and still to stay together.
I just want to feel better.

15. VEINS

He loves me,
He loves me not.
He loves me,
He loves me not.

The petals don't come easily off this yellow rose,
But as the pile on my desk grows,
An idle occupation,
I have a realization.

My fingers have always craved soft touches,
But as my thumb brushes
Over the petal, although it's thin
It feels something like skin.

The veins, the texture.
Now, I'm no expert
But don't I have veins, too?
I never thought it through.

I'm not sure what this feeling is,
But I've got the same thing running through my wrists.

16. WRITING IS READING

Brains put out what they take in,
That's the way it's always been.
No need to get dispirited;
These days, poetry's just another food in the pyramid.
Hierarchy of needs?
Please.
Like we don't need it all in equal measure.

17. SPIN APART

I can feel myself breaking down,
Making such a disjointed sound.
Wheels spinning so fast their steady whirs become a
high-pitched scream,
Throwing off sparks of light and steam.

Underneath the blur,
The splintering begins to occur.

Coming apart at the seams, spinning faster and faster,
Trying to outrun the fractures
Throwing out whatever's close
In the hopes it'll keep what matters most.
Fill in the gaps,
But speed just ups the pressure
And it
Begins
To c r a   c   k—

18. SLIDE

Spinning so much you know longer know which way is up,
Body melting in the chair.
There's no heads-up,
Barely aware

As you slide into sleep,
So slowly,
And deep,
You don't even notice the only

Border between awake and dreaming
Dissolve,
Seeming
Enthralled…

Until your head falls
And you jerk
Back to life like a doll
In the car, in the nighttime sand, at work.

19. EXILE

Words do not always flow
Trapped indoors at home
They need space to grow
So I roam.

Exile
At the end of the world
Or anywhere I can go for a while
And let my thoughts be unfurled.

20. EMBERS

Remember, remember,
Keep stoking the embers
In your heart.
Creativity is a part
Of you, don't let them go
And day by day, they'll grow.